Self-Publishing

Successfully

A 20-Step Guide

by Michael Williams

BIS Publications | T: +44 (0) 7903 791 469 | E: info@bispublications.com | Skype: bispub

Credits

Author: Michael Williams

Front Cover Design: Cindy Soso

Design & Layout: Jeorge Asare-Djan

Text Copyright © 2013 Michael Williams

Front Cover Design Copyright © 2013 Cindy Soso

Design & Layout Copyright © 2013 Jeorge Asare-Djan

First Published 2012

Second Edition June 2013

Third Edition 2014

ISBN: 978-1-903289-14-3

BIS Publications

T: +44 (0) 7903 791 469

web: www.bispublications.com

Skype: bispub

Acknowledgement

I would like to thank my publishing course training team:

Cindy, Sam, Jeorge and Chima,

for their dedication, help, and advice.

There Has Never Been A Better Time To Self Publish!

$\mathcal{D}$edication

This book is dedicated to all the authors and people in the book industry whom I have worked with in one way or another; to all those who have attended the various BIS Publishing Courses ™; to Cindy, Sam, Jeorge, Chima; to those who have attended my presentations; and to all those who dream of one day becoming a best-selling author.

$\mathcal{D}$ISCLAIMER

The advice contained in this material might not be suitable for everyone. The author designed the information to present his opinion about the subject matter. It is advised that the reader carefully investigate all aspects of any publishing decision before committing her or himself. The information contained is from the author's personal experience and sources the author considers reliable.

The author believes the information contained here is sound, but the reader cannot hold him responsible for either the actions they take or results of these actions.

*T*able of Contents

My Introduction

My name is Michael Williams, and I am the CEO of BIS Publications, a UK based publisher of children books. I am also the co-author of several books that have been rather successful over the years. I first started as a self-publishing author; my first title did very well nationally and internationally. I have gone on to self-publish many titles as well as publish books by other authors that continue to do well nationally and internationally.

During my 15 years in this industry, I have had many people ask me how I have been able to self-publish so many successful. Many of them want to give up their 9-to-5 jobs and write for a living, but they just don't know how to get started. With this in mind I created a course, based on my many years of experience as an author and publisher, designed to empower writers to produce best-selling books and reap the profits. Please note: You don't have to be the best writer in the world to have a widely read book or even a best-seller.

So

Don't you think it's time you stop thinking about one day writing a book?

Don't you think it's time you stop talking about one day writing a book?

Don't you think it's time you told your story and communicated it to the rest of the world?

Wouldn't you like to find out how you can make it happen?

If yes, then take **ACTION** and take it **NOW**!

If you are ready to take action, then this e-book is for you, and my 20 Steps to Successfully Self-Publishing will help that dream become a reality. Before we get started, let me say that you must believe in yourself even if everyone around doubts you. Don't allow other people to stop you from what you are destined to do. Even those closest to us can sometimes say the most negative things that can stop us in our tracks. They may say things such as: you can't do that; it's never been done before; no one wants to read anything that you have to say, let alone pay for it; or all you are going to do is waste your money on that course. We can accept this from strangers, but when it comes from friends or family, it can be devastating and may stop us from reaching our goals if we allow it.

Then there are the two little voices in our heads: one is our intuition which looks out for us; and the other is our self-doubt, a lack of confidence and self-worth which can cripple us. The trouble is identifying which is which. One makes us into great human beings allowing us to fulfil our potential and destiny; the other robs us of our destiny through comments such as "You can't do that!"

AND THEN THERE IS PROCRASTINATION

You all know what I mean: you say you'll start it tomorrow. Then tomorrow comes, but there is something you believe is more important that needs to be taken care of, so you say you'll start it next week. Then next week comes, and again you place more importance in something else and put off writing your book. By the third week, month, or year you start to feel guilty, so you justify to yourself why you haven't started by making excuses such as not having the time because of all the other things you had to complete. So you say you'll do it someday.

SOMEDAY?

Well, let me tell you now, "Someday" is not a day of the week! If you want to self-publish successfully, then you must start NOW! Not tomorrow, next week, or next month, but NOW!

Now that you're ready to start, I am going to give you my 20 Step Guide to Self-Publishing Successfully.

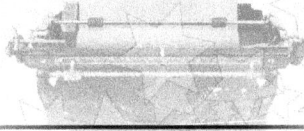

Why Do You Want To Write A Book?

think it's best to start at the beginning. Even before you put pen to paper you should ask yourself several questions. What is it that will compel or inspire me to sit down and write for hours, days, months, and possibly years?

It may be that you have a story to tell; it may be that you have always wanted to read a certain type of book but have never found it, because it has not been written yet. It may be that you would be so excited just to see your name on the front cover of a book. It may be that you have been caught up in all the J. K. Rowling, E.L. James, and Amanda Hocking hype, and you believe you could be the next great international best-selling author. It could be that you are self e-employed and believe a great way to educate your current and potential clients about your products and services would be through a book. It may be that you have worked in a particular industry for many years and have become an expert in that field, and you now want to teach others through a book.

Whatever your reasons are, you need to know that the self-publishing journey is not an easy one; it comes with many obstacles along the way, and if you are the type of person who quits at the first hurdle, then it's probably best that you don't start. But if you find that you have that burning desire to tell your STORY; to see it in print on paper or in pixels on screen; if you are willing to stand apart from the crowd; if you are willing to develop that idea from an inspiration to a fully fledged book; if you are willing to take criticisms, rejections, make mistakes and come back even stronger; and if you are willing to take that road of the less travelled, then you have what it takes to become a best-selling self-published author.

I can't promise you riches, but I can promise a challenge, an opportunity, enjoyment along the journey, and a sense of fulfilment, especially when a reader tells you how much they enjoyed your book, or how it's helped them and even changed their lives.

Please please do not get caught up in a paralysis of analysis or procrastination. I teach students in my courses to always have an exit strategy at every stage of their self-publishing journey. You should have one too, else you can waste a lot of time and not make the type of progress you desire.

$\mathcal{T}$IME

In the last 5 years I have seen a massive increase in authors who want to self-publish. Gone are the days when self-publishing was seen as inferior to being published by one of the 'Big Six'. The term vanity publishing is no longer scorned or seen as a dirty word. The big publishing houses now have some competition from smaller independents who have capitalized well on the use of new technologies. Large international online retailers such as Amazon (Kindle), Apple (iStore) and Google (Books) have also entered the field by not only retailing books, but also offering e-publishing solutions and a retail outlet for authors. When billionaire international best-selling author J.K. Rowling decides to self-publish in e-format the Harry Potter series directly from her web-site, you have to stop and take heed to what's going on in the book industry.

In my opinion, this industry has never gone through such dramatic change in such a short period of time: selling books online, digital printing, e-publishing, and of course new containers for reading books such as e-readers, tablets, and smart phones. Sales of e-book containers of all types have been growing at exponential rates for the last few years, and all evidence shows that trend will continue; this will translate into more people reading e-books. That said, I personally believe that the paper book is not dead; rather, I believe that the e-book will help the sales of paper books. It's also my belief if you have ever wanted to write a book, now is probably the best time to do so; there has never been a better time for the self-publishing author. Now you have to ask yourself if you're ready to join the journey of the best-selling authors.

What Is Self-Publishing?

1 The Idea (research)

•

2 Write

•

3 Publish (production)

•

4 Marketing and Sales (communicate the story)

•

"Self Publishing is all the four stages

carried out by the author"

P lease take careful note of stage four. Too many people fall short of achieving moderate book sales, let alone becoming best-selling authors simply because they do not take in account the final publishing stage. If you want to achieve great sales, then take the final stage seriously. I address this in both my online and offline courses as well as in my book *The Confessions of a Book Marketing Genius.*

The Michael Williams' Self Publisher Flow Chart™

The Essential Stages Involved in Publishing & Selling a Book Successfully

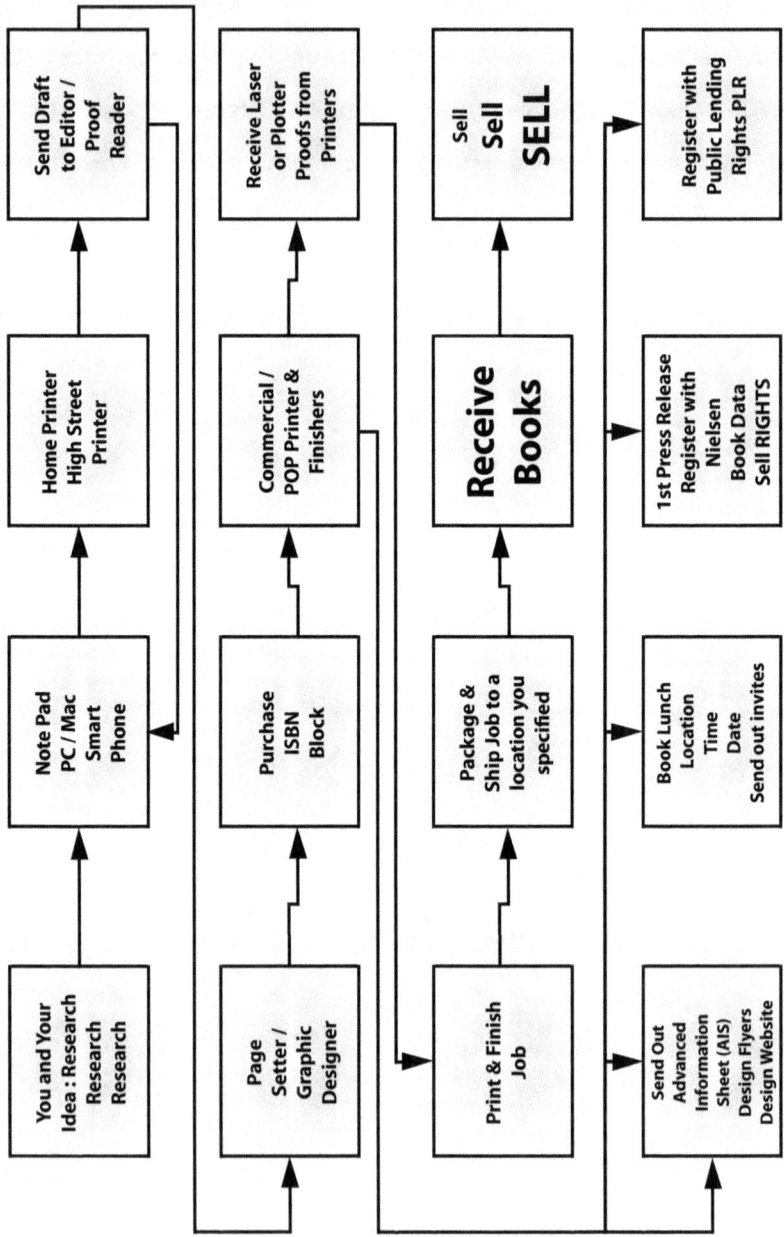

```
You and Your          Note Pad          Home Printer          Send Draft
Idea : Research        PC / Mac          High Street           to Editor /
Research               Smart             Printer               Proof
Research               Phone                                   Reader

Page                   Purchase          Commercial /          Receive Laser
Setter /               ISBN              POP Printer &         or Plotter
Graphic                Block             Finishers             Proofs from
Designer                                                       Printers

Print & Finish         Package &         Receive               Sell
Job                    Ship Job to a     Books                 Sell
                       location you                            SELL
                       specified

Send Out               Book Lunch        1st Press Release     Register with
Advanced               Location          Register with         Public Lending
Information            Time              Nielsen               Rights PLR
Sheet (AIS)            Date              Book Data
Design Flyers          Send out invites  Sell RIGHTS
Design Website
```

UK BIS Publications 1 Day Intensive course for African Caribbean writers who want to Self Publish Successfully

BIS Publications 16 June 2011 © Copyright 2011 Michael Williams

$\mathcal{J}$UST START

Too many people don't start their self-publishing project simply because they are too afraid of failing. Little do they know that they have already failed if they won't start. Make sure that you don't become one of these people. Remember that everyone fails at some thing or another; failing is not a problem, it only becomes a problem if we fail to learn from what we fail at. I have learned that there is always a golden nugget to be found in almost everything that I have failed.

Apart from Just Start, the next most important part of your self- publishing journey will be the utilization of my Focus, Concentrate, and Believe (F.C.B.) formula.

Please see the mathematical formula below.

F = Focus, C = Concentrate and B = Believe

Therefore

(F + C) x B = GS (Great Success).

So Get FOCUSED

CONCENTRATE

On the matter at hand. You must do this to the point where your book project takes priority over almost everything, and at times you are conscious of nothing else. A strong desire to successfully complete your book plus a concentrated effort should give your desired result.

BELIEVE

With all your heart and soul that you can and will produce your own published book successfully. This is where you must become a best-selling author in your own head before you actually see it happen in real life. What I mean by this is that you start acting like a best seller: you tell your self every day that you are a best seller and you are in the process of producing another best selling book. By doing this you are setting up the conditions to make it possible for you to be successful; you are also creating a positive energy that will allow your thoughts and ideas to flow. Your writing will also be better and you will prevent, or at least reduce, writer's block.

'Faith without works is dead' - James 2:20-22

FOCUS

On completing your writing project the best analogy I can use to describe focus is to liken it to when a child holds a piece of paper up to the sun on a sunny day and hopes for it to catch fire. Of course we know it won't catch fire, but once that child employs a magnifying glass and then directs those sun rays onto that paper, all of a sudden the paper starts to smoulder, catches a light, and burns. That's the type of focus I'm talking about.

Put your ideas down on paper. It is very important that you research your market thoroughly. If you want to produce a best-selling title, then it's imperative that you know the **TRUE** facts about your market niche and not just the opinions of a few; or worse, just guessing that the book might have buyers. When you research and get all the necessary data, you will feel much more confident and certain on how well your book will do. So **RESEARCH**, **RESEARCH** and then **RESEARCH** some more.

When writing a book, make sure you title it in such a way that it has market appeal. What's in a name? Everything! We have all heard the old adage "Don't judge a book by its cover"; unfortunately, many of us do and the book title is part of the cover. So remember that the cover and its title are your shop window to the content within the cover pages.

Note: A great way to develop an idea is to **THINK**. To think creates mental energy it stimulates the **MIND** which can produces desired results. The problem is most people have never done it.

"Thinking is the hardest work there is, which is probably the reason why so few engage in it." - Henry Ford

Step #1
Reminder

You And Your Ideas

●

Concentrate

●

Focus

●

Believe

●

Research, Research, Research

Step #2

WRITE, TYPE, TALK, AND RECORD

There is no excuse not to put your ideas down on paper. The advancements made in technology during this century have allowed us to convey our ideas in much easier and affordable ways and are accessible for almost everyone. What we can do today, we simply were not able to do just a few years ago. For example, 20 years ago, most of us did not have a typewriter at home and did not have access to one. Today, most of us have access to a much more powerful device, the computer, at home, work, or our local internet café and library.

Wherever I am in the world I now meet people who have at least one or more cell phones. Smart phones have word processing capabilities that can be used for jotting down ideas and even writing a whole book.

Some of you may hate writing and would rather just tell your story. There are products on the market, including basic smart phones and computers, which will allow you to read aloud your story and it will be automatically typed.

Finally, if that does not rock your boat, you can always employ a ghost writer to write your book. No, these are not spooks; they are usually freelance writers who are happy to write other people's books for a fee while the author keeps all the rights. What I'm trying to say is whatever way you do it, just do it!

Step #2
Reminder

Note Pad

•

Pc / Mac

•

Smart Phone

•

Tape / Digital Recorders

$\mathscr{S}$*tep* #3

$\mathscr{E}$*DIT*

O nce your manuscript is typed, you can do the first edits. Getting your edits correct can determine the success of your book. Because of the ease of self-publishing today, many people are publishing poor quality work, which, in many cases, results in poor sales. Avoid this by taking this step very seriously.

I always believe that the first edits are best done by you as in the end it will save you time and money.

Step #4

PROOFREAD

O nce you finish your edits and are happy with what you have done, find a good proof reader and editor. I believe using a freelance editor who does editing for a living is best. My cautionary **NOTE**, if your budget is tight and you are trying to save money, you may consider using family members or friends; if so, Seek objectivity! Only show friends and family your work when nearly complete. I give reasons for this in my other self-publishing books.

When you receive your work back from the editor, try it on an objective audience, not family members. With feedback from the audience, make last minute changes. Please note at every stage it's important not to get caught up in the paralysis of analysis; this is just another form of procrastination. I have seen this first hand over the years when I have worked with authors, many of whom never complete their book.

'There are some people that are so negative that when they go into a dark room they start to develop' - Les Brown

Step #5

COPYRIGHT

Now that your copy is right, protect it. Many authors feel it is important to protect their copyright; some are terrified of sending their manuscript out to a proof reader/editor for fear that their work will be copied. So for those of you who need the security that your work is protected, continue reading the next paragraph.

For now, just to make you more confident about showing your work without the fear of anyone stealing it, you can follow this simple process. Enclose a copy of your manuscript in an envelope and send it to yourself in the post recorder delivery. Never open it unless you need to contest copyright for infringement in a court of law. Now that was easy, wasn't it?

Make sure on your title/credits page, you put the word "copyright", including the symbol (©), your name, and the date. In my book, Confessions of a Best-Selling Self-Published Author, I go in to more detail about several types of intellectual property, which includes copyright.

*S*tep #6

*P*ROOFREAD

Send to a professional proof reader / editor. I know I have already said this in step 4, but this step is for all those authors who were worried about their copyright and would not send it out until they felt protected. If you have completed step 5, it's time to complete step 4.

Steps #3 to 6
Reminder

Self Edit Manuscript

•

Proofread

•

Copyright Book

•

Have Book Edited &
Proofread by Professional

$\mathscr{S}$tep #7

$\mathscr{D}$ESIGN

When your edits are finished and you're happy with your manuscript, it's time to find a good graphic designer or typesetter.

The choice between typesetter and graphic designer depends on the type of book you're producing. Generally speaking, employ a typesetter if your book is an autobiography or adult fiction, and a graphic designer if it's a children's book, coffee table book, or cookbook. Regardless of what genre your book falls in, you will need a graphic designer for your front and back cover. Most graphic designers can do what typesetters do, but most typesetters can't do what graphic designers can.

If you are trained in any of the above areas, you can always do it yourself to save money. On the other hand, if, like most of us, you can just about draw a box on a computer, then it's best you leave your book layout and design to the professionals.

Once you have the answers to your questions and know which route you will take, find a printing company or e-book company that serves your needs. You should inquire at several and get several quotes before choosing the one for you.

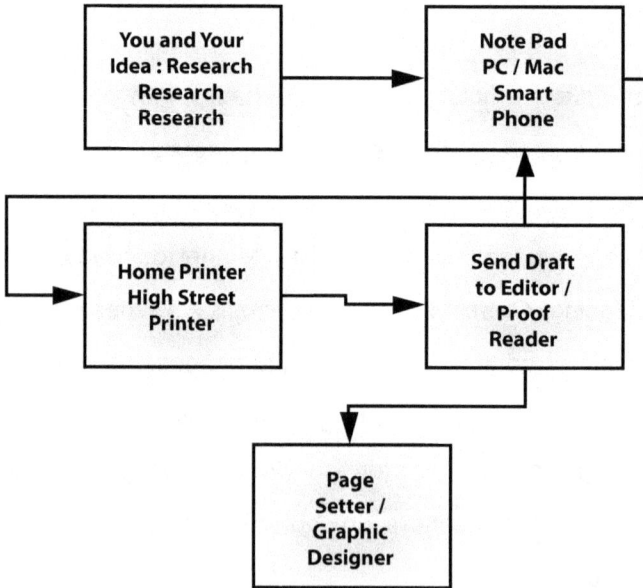

```
┌─────────────────┐           ┌─────────────────┐
│  You and Your   │           │    Note Pad     │
│ Idea : Research  │─────────▶ │    PC / Mac     │
│    Research     │           │     Smart       │
│    Research     │           │     Phone       │
└─────────────────┘           └─────────────────┘

┌─────────────────┐           ┌─────────────────┐
│  Home Printer   │           │   Send Draft    │
│  High Street    │─────────▶ │   to Editor /   │
│    Printer      │           │     Proof       │
│                 │           │     Reader      │
└─────────────────┘           └─────────────────┘

                    ┌─────────────────┐
                    │      Page       │
                    │    Setter /     │
                    │    Graphic      │
                    │    Designer     │
                    └─────────────────┘
```

$\mathcal{S}$tep #8

$\mathcal{F}$ORMAT

Now that your book is laid out, it is time to decide how your book will be published. There are two main ways we read books today: the traditional p-book (paper book) and the e-book (electronic book).

If you choose to publish as a p-book, then it will be important to know the quantity of books you want printed. Armed with that knowledge, you'll be better equipped in choosing whether to use a digital (on demand) printer or a lithographic offset printer. I talk about the difference and pros and cons of these two methods of printing in my book Confessions of a Best-Selling Self-Published Author.

If you choose to publish as an e-book, you will need to get good advice from professionals in that area and ask them several questions. One such question is what type of devices can your e-book be read on? For example, can it be read on a computer, e-reader, tablet, or smart phone? Other questions are once it's in an e-format, can it be easily copied? How do I protect it? And how and where do I sell e-books?

Steps #7 to 8
Reminder

Consider Your Design Approach

•

Consider Your Format Choice

•

P-Book , E-Book
or Both

*I*SBN

Register for an International Standard Book Number (ISBN) certificate and purchase one or a block of ISBN numbers. A block usually consists of 10 ISBN numbers in the UK; the blocks or amount may differ in other countries.

ISBN 978-3-16-148410-0

9 783161 484100 >

EAN / BARCODE

Purchase a barcode, sometimes referred to as an (International) European Article Number (EAN); the EAN is generated from your ISBN. The EAN-13 is a 13-digit unique code for your product represented by scanable bars. Shops and libraries will use it for their computerized stock control system.

0   123456 789012

𝒮tep #11

ℛEGISTER

Register with Nielsen Book Data so distributors, shops, and libraries will be able to order and stock your book(s). In the US, you may also want to register with Bowkers; in other countries there may be other agencies which are more applicable to the region in which you are selling your book.

If your book has only been published as an e-book, you are not required to have an ISBN or EAN, but you may want to have a Quick Response (QR) Code. We speak about this in my other title.

$\mathscr{S}$tep #12

$\mathscr{S}$UBMISSION

If you have chosen the p-book route, once you have found your preferred printer, send them your manuscript electronically. This is because if it is a hard copy and the printer has to retype and design your book, your costs will go up significantly. Also, you want it to be electronic so that either you or the printer can make last minute changes easily, quickly, and cost effectively. Please make sure you include the ISBN and EAN.

It is very important to get proofs back from the printer before they do the final print. As a self-publishing author, there's nothing worse than paying for 5000 books that are incorrect.

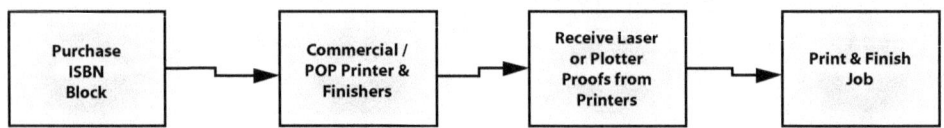

Purchase ISBN Block	→	Commercial / POP Printer & Finishers	→	Receive Laser or Plotter Proofs from Printers	→	Print & Finish Job

Steps #9 to 12
Reminder

Isbn / Ean

•

Register with Nielsen Book Data

•

Printers & Finishers

•

Recieve Proofs Before Printing

•

Print & Finish Job

Step #13

*M*ARKET

Start your marketing and sales campaign. But I hear you say you can't sell. It's not that you can't sell, it's just that you won't sell. The reason you will not get up and sell is because you haven't created a big enough **WHY** to sell. If you want to have successful book sales, it's not so much knowing the How.

It's more about the **WHY**.

If your **WHY** is **BIG** enough, you will do whatever it takes to make great sales happen.

On my course *"How To Market Your Book And Create The Demand"* and in my title *The Confessions of a Book Marketing Genius*, I give strategies on how to best market and sell your book. So do join me the next time our courses are running; alternatively, pick up the above title.

Step #14

ADVANCE INFORMATION SHEET

As part of marketing, send out an Advance Information Sheet (AIS) to bookshops, wholesalers, and book distributors. This should be sent out up to nine months before your book is published. The AIS is simply an A4 sheet of paper with the description of your book.

It should include the book's dimensions, page numbers, cover type (hard back or soft back), genre, author(s) name, illustrator(s) name, ISBN, due publication date, publisher, price, and picture of the front cover. It should also include a short synopsis and a short bio of you, the author.

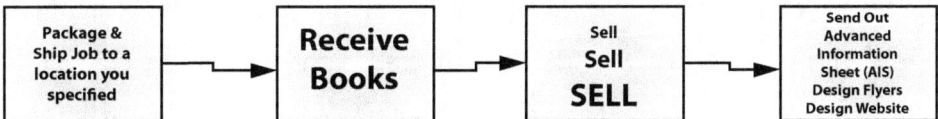

Package & Ship Job to a location you specified	Receive Books	Sell Sell SELL	Send Out Advanced Information Sheet (AIS) Design Flyers Design Website

$\mathscr{S}tep$ #15

$\mathscr{A}$NNOUNCEMENT

Plan and prepare your book launch. This is your announcement to the market; it is an advertisement that your book has arrived - so make some **NOISE!**

Step #16 $\mathscr{C}$ONTACT DISTRIBUTORS / WHOLESALERS

Contact several distributors and ask if they will purchase books from you. This is usually a 50%-60% discount; credit arrangements are normally for 30, 60, or 90 days. Remember there is no set rule -- it is all negotiable, so learn and practice negotiating.

You can find book wholesalers and distributors by visiting trade shows, searching the internet, and asking a bookseller to recommend a distributor. A word of warning, make sure you find a distributor/ wholesaler who understands your market.

Don't forget, when selling your book, the wholesaler, distributor, and even the book seller is not the be all and end all. Due to mass advancements in information technology, we all now have a very powerful marketing and sales tool (the computer and internet) that can be utilised to sell directly to an end customer. This cuts out the middleman, and you get to keep all the profits.

You can also sell directly at your own events, seminars, and workshops.

Step #17 MARKET

Design flyers, business cards, bookmarks, and website, blog, Facebook, etc, to market your book.

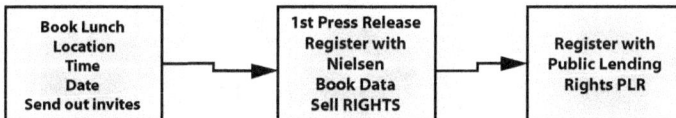

Book Lunch Location Time Date Send out invites	→	1st Press Release Register with Nielsen Book Data Sell RIGHTS	→	Register with Public Lending Rights PLR

Steps #*13 to 17*
Reminder

*S*ell, Sell, Sell

•

*S*end Out Advanced Information Sheet (AIS)

•

*P*lan Book Launch

•

*C*ontact Distributors / Wholesalers

•

*M*arket Your Book

𝒮tep #18

𝒜DVERTISE

Send advance copies to the media, book groups, and anyone who has a large following or audience that will talk about your book. You might be able to get free advertisement (in the form of an editorial) in a local or even national newspaper if they think the story both in and out of the book is good enough, so make sure you also sell yourself.

If you have testimonials, then you should have several excerpts included on the back cover of your book; testimonials can go a long way in selling your book.

Step #19 𝒫ERSEVERE

Keep pushing - never, Never, **NEVER EVER GIVE UP**, until you know you have given your very best, yes **YOUR VERY BEST**.

Step #20
Remember the Formula

Believe

•

Concentrate

•

& Focus

Steps #*18 to 20*
Reminder

Advertise

•

Persevere

•

& Remember the Formula

Well done!

You are now on your way!

Remember that 80% of **Success**

is in **"STARTING"**.

Some Final Notes To Authors

ORIGINALITY

Originality usually sets apart the wheat from the chaff. There are hundreds of thousands of new titles being published and self-published every day by both new and established authors. Somehow, you will have to get your book seen amongst the plethora of all these titles. When I say originality, I mean not just the narrative within the covers of your book, but also the narrative outside the covers. That will include an original concept for your book cover, your sales copy on the flyer promoting your book, the copy written on your website or other websites selling your book, and generally your overall marketing strategy. It is said that the cream always floats to the top; make sure that your book is amongst the cream.

CONSISTENCY

Your book must be consistent. Therefore, if there are page numbers, make sure the pages are correctly numbered throughout the book and that the numbers appear in the same place throughout the book. This is also true for chapter headings and subtitles. If chapter one is at the top centre of the page, then make sure chapters 2, 3, 4, etc. follow in the same way. In terms of the content (story), if you are writing a piece which includes a character's name that appears several times in the story, then be consistent here also; spell the name the same way throughout the book, less you confuse your reader.

*F*ILE & FORMAT

It is imperative that you know what file types and format your printer or e-book provider uses. There is nothing worse than having a finished book saved as a file type or formatted a certain way only to find that your printer or e-publisher provider does not work with that file or style of format.

Over the years, I have found that most printers do not like to work with Microsoft Publisher. It is best to stick to software such as Microsoft Word or any software that can create high quality PDF files.

My Why

Why I want to write and self publish?

Knowledge + Application + Accountability + Motivation

Where are you now with your book?

_____

_____

_____

_____

_____

_____

Answer / Steps / Solutions / Plan

_____

_____

_____

_____

_____

What has held me back until now?

Where do yo want to be in terms of your book?

_____

_____

_____

_____

_____

_____

_____

_____

Glossary Of Terms

POD = Print on Demand

PDF = Portable Document File

ISBN = International Standard Book Number

EAN = European Article Number renamed the International Article Number

Lithographic Offset printer = A type of print technology that is the standard for printing books

Digital Printing = A print technology that allows short print-runs and can be cost effective for self-publishing authors.

P- Book = A paper formatted book

E - Book = An electronic formatted book.

www.ingramcontent.com/pod-product-compliance
Lightning Source LLC
La Vergne TN
LVHW051712080426
835511LV00017B/2877